Garden of the Heart

They Do Not Understand Series

Patricia C. Vines

Copyright @2016

Patricia C. Vines

All rights reserved. No part of this book may be reproduced or transmitted in any form or by any means, electronic or mechanical, including photocopying, recording, or by any information storage and retrieval system, without permission in writing from the copyright owner or author.

The information in this book is for educational purposes only.

ISBN-13: 978-1530294664
ISBN-10: 1530294665

First Edition
Printed in the United States of America

Table of Contents

Introduction iv
Acknowledgments vi
Rose 1
Gardenia 4
Daffodil 6
Iris 8
Pansy 9
Camellia 11
Pond Lily 13
Resurrection Lily 15
Bleeding Heart 17
Sunflower 18
Poppy 21
Daisy 25
Tube Rose 26
Forget-Me-Not 28
Chrysanthemum 29
Cosmos 31
Gladiola 33
Carnation 34
Marigold 37
Brown-Eyed Susan 39
Aster 41
Petunia 43
Nasturtium 44
Blue Delphinium 46
Violet 47
Orchid 50
7 Feast Of The LORD Being Symbolic Of New Life 53

Introduction

This "Garden of the Heart" has no definite plan of arrangement. Surely there should come the privilege of professing an understanding of God's plan and purpose for flowers. To see God's Word in them, the only requirement is to look, listen and touch. They are God's thoughts of beauty, his whispers of courage, his messages of love, his Spirit taking shape to gladden mortal gaze. Each little petal dancing in the breeze is but the smile of Eternal Goodness.

Sometimes it seems almost a pity that they can make no sound. How fine it would be to have a singing rose, a laughing larkspur, a murmuring marigold, a chatting cosmos, a whispering violet, a pleading pansy, a cheering carnation, or a tinkling tulip!

Upon such musing there dawns the consciousness that, though they cannot speak audibly when words fail man he uses them to express his deepest emotions. One writes upon a slip of paper or even engraves upon the finest card "Heartfelt sympathy," or "Dearest Love," or Heartiest congratulations," or some other expression of tender feeling, then stand off to view it. How inadequate it seems to transmit the surging of the heart! But wait, they are Love's truest language as they wreathe the cradle, the diploma, the marriage altar, the sick room, etc. Walk into a grocery store and the flowers yearn to be touched and caressed, just a simple touch of adoration at God's glorious beauty.

To strive to analyze the charm of a flower is like dissecting music. It is far better to enjoy them, to touch each petal, to revel in their beauty and fragrance than to make any attempt fully to understand them. It is more satisfying to look upon each blossom as an autograph from the hand of God upon the world about everyone. Not fully understanding them, forever seeking to fathom the depth and height, the length and breadth of their appeal, always approaching them with head uncovered in the consciousness of treading on holy ground, one stands before these loved expressions of Deity with humility and gratitude. Truly, they are masterpieces of God, these lovely jewels of nature, these bright gems of earth. In them, perhaps, one glimpses what Eden was and what Paradise may be

John 16:13;
13 But when he, the Spirit of truth, comes, he will guide you into all the truth. He will not speak on his own; he will speak only what he hears, and he will tell you what is yet to come. (NIV®)

Acknowledgments

GOD'S WORD ® Translation is a registered trademark of GOD'S WORD® to the Nations, PO Box 400, Orange Park, Florida 32067-0400.

"Scripture quotations taken from the New American Standard Bible®, Copyright© 1960, 1962, 1963, 1968, 1971, 1972, 1973, 1975, 1977, 1995 by The Lockman Foundation Used by permission." (www.Lockman.org)

Scripture quotations are taken from the HOLY BIBLE, New Living Translation, copyright© 1996, 2004, 2007, 2013 by Tyndale House Foundation. Used by permission of Tyndale House Publishers, Inc., Carol Stream, Illinois 60188. All rights reserved.

Some of the Scripture quotations, in this publication are from the HOLY BIBLE, NEW INTERNATIONAL VERSION® NIV® Copyright© 1973, 1978, 1984, 2011 by Biblica, Inc.®. Used by permission. All rights reserved worldwide. The "NIV" and "New International Version" are trademarks registered in the United States Patent and Trademark Office by Biblica, Inc.®. Use of either trademark requires the permission of Biblica, Inc.®.

"Scripture quotations are from The Holy Bible, English Standard Version® (ESV®), copyright© 2001 by Crossway, a publishing ministry of Good News Publishers. Used by permission. All rights reserved."

Scripture quotations marked HCSB are taken from the Holman Christian Standard Bible®, Copyright© 1999, 2000, 2002, 2003 by Holman Bible Publishers. Used by permission. Holman Christian Standard Bible®, Holman CSB®, and HCSB® are federally registered trademarks of Holman Bible Publishers.

Scripture taken from the New King James Version®. Copyright© 1982 by Thomas Nelson, Inc. Used by permission. All rights reserved.

NET Bible copyright © 1996-2006 by Biblical Studies Press, L.L.C. http://netbible.com.

All pictures and information contained therein in this book is factual to the best of the author information and is presented for informational and entertainment purposes only.

Rose

Apostle Paul closes his matchless thirteenth chapter of 1 Corinthians with these stirring often quoted words: **"And now abideth faith, hope, love, these three; and the greatest of these is love."** The greatest of these is love! Indeed this is well-spoken, for love is God, and God is love.

Love is the great motivating power, the dynamic urge which inspired, indwelt and, instigated the Father, Son, and Holy spirit as the wondrous holy trinity, hungry for the human touch and response, said, **""Let us make man in our image, after our likeness." Genesis 1:26.** When man through sin fell from this high estate, thus placing an insurmountable barrier between himself and God, again love it was which sought a remedy and sent the beloved son to open up a new and living way to the father for those who sought through faith in him to regain communion and devotion.

Can there be a blossom found to tell of this marvelous grace? Yes, there is one which continually breathes it, for it is the universal message and messenger of *love*. When I want to tell he Lord how much I adore him, I use the language of love in the Song of Songs. This beautiful book of the Bible is more than just a love poem; it is a picture of the love relationship between the bridegroom and his bride. **"Neither height nor depth, nor anything else in all creation, will be able to separate us from the love of God that is in Christ Jesus our Lord. Romans 8:39.**

One morning during the happy school teaching days of young womanhood, a little girl came rushing into my room with a bunch of beautiful red roses clutched in her tiny hands. Unable to wait until reaching the desk to joyfully present them, she cried out, "Miss Patricia, do you know what red roses say?"

After many years this teacher still feels the shame and chagrin of answering, "No."

"Why," said Hilda, "Miss Patricia, red roses say, 'I love you!'"

Yes, red roses say, "I love you!" not only red roses but also every rose that ever has or ever will lift its radiant face to the sun, every rose that ever has or ever will grace any experience of joy or sorrow sings this wondrous hymn of love.

What a fitting symbol this God-given thing of beauty is for our love for one another! John said, **"Beloved, let us love one another: for love is of God; and every one that loveth is born of God, and knoweth God" 1 John 4:7.**

It graciously pictures the outreach of the human heart to him in adoration. It sets forth in bold relief mortal affection, in essence truly divine, yet so apt to waver, so often to neglect, and sometimes even to forget the glorious object of such devotion.

However, the climax of the heart message, of this miracle of creation, the radiant rose, is its message of God's love for man.

There is nothing strange in the fact that man loves God. The unbelievable thing is that anyone who hears of him can ever fail to love him who is Love. It is unthinkable to ponder the truth that so many have and will reject him who in love gave his life for each of them. How can anyone ever hear of Jesus and turn away from his loving offer?

The marvel of the whole plan is that he first loved us. **"We love him, because he first loved us" 1 John 4:19.** The Heavenly Father looked down upon man; lost; undone, unlovely, steeped in guilt, and reaching out to him in his sin and shame,

> In loving kindness Jesus came
> My soul in mercy to reclaim
> And from the depths of sin and shame,
> Thro' grace He lifted me.

Charlotte G. Homer

As the devoted heart bows in humility at the wonder of it all, reverently he breathes the query, **"Why should he love me so?"**

One word more the rose would add before completing its little sermonette. Surely it would say, **"Before leaving me, look more closely upon my structure. Look beyond the radiance of my beauty, beyond the delicacy of my texture, and what do you see?"**

Yes, there they are, easily discerned with the naked eye, poignantly revealed to the touch, the thorns. How true the saying, **"Every rose has its thorns."**

Just so, the path of Christian love is not always smooth, not always easy. It has its thorns. Jesus said, **"If any man will come after me, let him deny himself, and take up his cross daily, and follow me" Luke 9:23.**

In the way the believer must tread there is always a cross. He must take up his own cross. How he misunderstands this at times! How often does he dub some chastisement brought on by willfulness and sin a cross! He forgets that **"God is not mocked: for whatsoever a man soweth, that shall he also reap." Galatians 6:7.** Never be guilty of calling that which is sown in the flesh, and is of the flesh reaping corruption, a tree (cross). One real look at the tree (cross) of Calvary makes the Christian hesitate to call any earthly experience, however painful, a tree (cross).

The tree (cross) in the believer's life is saying "No" to his own desires, purposes, and plans, however lofty they may be, and saying "Yes" to God's will, whatever denial it may demand from the earthly viewpoint. Then, just as the waters of Marah were made sweet when Moses cast the tree into them, so when Golgaotha's tree and the redemption it brought finds its place in the human heart, every experience is made sweet for its being there. Only then have we **"Known and believed the love that God hath to us. God is love; and he** that dwelleth in love dwelleth in God, and God in him" 1 John 4:16.

Surely it is no mere coincidence that the rose, called by some the queen of all the flowers, should manifest the highest virtue of the King of all creation. **"Love the LORD your God with all your heart and with all your soul and with all your strength." Deuteronomy 6:5.**

Gardenia

There is one flower, beautiful beyond expression, fragrant, too, which apparently has everything in itself, and yet its heart message seems a thing standing between it and a larger usefulness. The flower is the "Gardenia," and its message is that of *sensitiveness.* **"Blessed is the man who does no walk in the counsel of the wicked or stand in the way of sinners or sit in the seat of mockers. But his delight is in the law of the LORD, and on his law he meditates day and night. He is like a tree planted by streams of water, which yields its fruit in season and whose leaf does nor wither. Whatever he does prospers. Psalm 1:1-3.**

To be sure, as Addison once said, there is a quick sensitiveness which is inseparable from understanding. Then again, one is reminded that petty slights are often harder to bear than real injury and can cause untold heartache. Being mindful of the fact the men have often died from the festering of a gnat's bite, there would surely be no thought of minimizing the havoc that can be wrought by such.

It is a super-sensitiveness that the gardenia speaks of, a quality which is closely allied with egotism (EGO) – Edging God Out, though neither our pretty flower nor a friend of like characteristic would admit such.

Pause for a moment and run back through the files of your memory. Find the first gardenia you ever saw. Remember what an object of beauty and perfection it was.

Perfect in formation, exquisite in texture, filling the room with its fragrance, robed in its spotless waxen dress, so lovely that the glory of it almost hurt. Irresistibly you felt drawn to it. You were impelled to touch its petal; and the touch was ever so light, a veritable gesture of affection. Furthermore, you almost instinctively leaned forward for a deeper aroma of its fragrance. Each move was one beyond any willing, and was a tribute of admiration and respect for the work of the divine Artist.

Did the gardenia accept your homage as given? Oh, no! There was an immediate withdrawal, and in this withdrawal it was outwardly marred by its sensitiveness. Yellow spots discolored its waxen surface. It was permanently marked in such a way as to bar its highest usefulness. Marred and marked by an impulsive deed in which there was never a thought or desire to harm, but breathing on it caused.

Scarcely will one think of such an incident without being led further in contemplation to say, *"That reminds me of So-and-So."* Then upon the memory scene will flash the vision of some friend or acquaintance, possibly some co-worker in some phase of life. In the musing, all his attractive qualities parade before the mind, his ability, personality, intellect, personal charm, seemingly everything to equip him for a worthy life in the Master's vineyard; and yet because of super-sensitiveness that friend lost his usefulness, blighted and discolored his testimony by harboring imaginary hurts which had no real foundation, or, if they did, those foundations were laid in innocent but misunderstood motives of love. **"You created my inmost being; you knit me together in my mother's womb. I praise you because I am fearfully and wonderfully made; your works are wonderful, I know that full well. Psalm 139:13-14.**

To one whose mind is stayed on Jesus, there is a constant reminder of his selflessness. He said of himself that he came not to be ministered unto but to minister. He did not allow himself to be swayed or hindered or marred in his work by what man said or thought, but he steadfastly went about his Father's business and finished his program. He was willing to spend and be spent, unmindful of self but with a loving heart ever reaching out to others.

In doing so, he demonstrated the truth that real beauty is not a thing of outward show, one which can so easily be marked and discolored, but it is the outgrowth of a surrendered life in whose heart the Lord Christ (Yeshua) reigns supreme. **"How precious to me are your thoughts, O God! How vast is the sum of them! Were I to count them, they would outnumber the grains of sand. When I awake, I am still with you. Psalm 139:17-18.**

Daffodil

Back in the happy high school days, among the many types of entertainment brought to the school was one which has never ceased to echo in the heart. It was the program of the Swiss Bell Ringers.

They were attractive because they were unusual, interesting because their quaint costumes, but they were remembered most of all for the harmony of their music and the clearness of the bells.

Amid the many blooms with which nature adorns the earth is a group which seems to be springs bell ringers, for truly they resemble dainty golden bells, and their mission seems to be to herald this welcome season. Have you already guessed their name? The daffodil, of course.

Even before the winter's fires are allowed to fade, before warm garments are replaced by lighter ones, or the blankets are laid on the shelf, these cheery, warm-hearted, bell-like blooms suddenly pop up everywhere to remind one that spring is actually just around the corner.

It would not be possible to hum the air of their song, but the words in their heart are easily discernible. They are lines from one of the greatest songs of all ages:

> Lo, the winter is past...
> the flowers appear on the earth.
> The time of the singing of birds is come.
> **Song of Solomon 2:11-12**

The daffodil seems to be assuring the world that the biting, wintry blasts, the cold, penetrating rains, the days of slippery sleet, and the beautiful yet sometimes treacherous blanket of snow have all, for a time, folded their tents like the Arabs and as silently stolen away.

Nor does the lovely herald stop with this word. It seems to bend closer that it may ring clearly its message to every troubled soul. Its chimes ring out above the disappointments, doubts, discouragements, distresses, and disasters of this sin-sick world. It urges one to keep his head unbowed against the chilling blasts of injustice, the penetrating rains of hate, the slippery days of conceit and self-satisfaction, the oft-time outwardly attractive but always treacherous paths of wickedness, but ever to keep his heart held high.

The daffodil constantly seeks to remind that the dark experiences are but for a season and beyond them is all the warmth, the joy, and the glory of spiritual spring in the heart. It heralds the glad news of victory to every believing soul, the blessed assurance that Jesus traveled every wintry path first, that he was tempted and tried at every point just as we are, but that he came forth from every somber experience into the light and glow and glory of eternal spring.

Because Christ lives in us, we can be filled with delight day after day. And those things that can and will delight us have nothing to do with position or ministry We can have delight in the dull, monotonous months, in the routine, mundane days, in the lean, hungry years. There are two verses in Proverbs: **"I was filled with delight day after day, rejoicing always in his presence, rejoicing in his whole world and delighting in mankind. Proverbs 8:30-31.**

In this suffering he bought not only redemption for every

trusting heart but also everlasting happiness and joy in the Golden City (Jerusalem) whose colors the dainty daffodil wears and whose welcome it rings out.

Iris

One of the most admirable flowers which grows is the iris. Approaching it, the writer confesses a tendency to timidity, a feeling of reticence in the presence of such dignity, for *dignity* is the message of its heart. One would no more go near it with familiarity than he would rush into the presence of the President of the United States with a "Hi Pal" on his lips.

Standing in its stately splendor, the iris seems to typify some bejeweled dowager looking down her nose through her lorgnette at the lesser lights about her or else some pompous squire with sideburns. Are you thinking, *"How silly thus to describe so beautiful a flower!"* One hastens to explain no offense is meant. Never would one be guilty of disparaging the incomparable iris. It is simply to say that in its dignity the iris seems to stand alone.

If other flowers could speak, particularly the smaller ones that are sometimes grouped in flower arrangements with the iris, they would probably confess that they do not feel quite comfortable and that the certain homey feeling of familiarity is absent from the group. Not that the iris did anything to cause such sentiment. Oh, no! It is far above snobbishness or pretense in any form. Its quiet, innate dignity unconsciously created such feelings.

Again, if the iris could speak, one ventures the opinion it would say that it did not enjoy being made into a corsage. It might confess to a hurt pride when its staunch stem and its stately leaves were cut from it, as though it felt undressed and thus bereft of its dignity.

It calls to mind Vashti. Do you remember her? One could almost wish the iris were named for her.

Vashti passed on and off the stage of Bible history in one short chapter. Her story is recounted quickly and briefly in order to reach the heroine of the story, Esther. However, she left an indelible impress on every thinking heart.

Vashti was the Queen, the wife of King Ahasuerus, the ruler of Media and Persia. She was beautiful and fair to look upon.

In the third year of his reign, Ahasuerus made a feast for all the princes and noblemen of his provinces. When it had continued seven days and had become a drunken debauch, he decided to bring the Queen before his guests that her beauty might be paraded before them and made sport of.

Vashti refused to obey the command of her lord and master, knowing full well the consequence of her disobedience, the loss of her position as Queen. She preferred to lose her exalted place in the kingdom rather than forfeit her dignity and self-respect.

Though the iris cannot speak for itself and is sometimes arranged beneath its dignity, even in such position its message to the world is self-evident.

Pansy

"Pansies for thoughts" is a saying familiar to everyone. To look into a pansy bed and see all the happy little faces, heads cocked to one side a pensive look on each little countenance as they muse, reminds one of the words of Plato, *"Thinking is the talking of the soul with itself."* **An anxious heart weights a man down, but a kind word cheers him up. Proverbs 12:25.**

Yes, here is something in such designation of this little flower. To look upon its blossoms sends one's mind back to Spurgeon's words: *"Good thoughts like flower petals give out sweet odor if laid up in the jar of memory."* Then again the admonition is heard to guard one's thoughts since they are heard in heaven. Encouragement has never filled a flat tire.

Encouragement has never made a car payment, not fixed a broken washing machine. But encouragement from another gives us the strength to do what we feel we cannot do, hold on when we feel we cannot hold on, and try what we might not dare to try. Encouragement. Does not sound like much, but it is everything. Sending encouragement will be a part of someone's memories for a long, long time.

Truly there seems to be something mental about the interesting little pansy. It seems more human than any other flower. However, it does not satisfy merely to say, *"Pansies for thought,"* because some thoughts are idle, scattered, and useless. The message of the pansy seems to be that of intelligent, concerted *thinking.*

Just outside Newman there is one of Georgia's loveliest flower plots, the Dunaway Gardens. Those who make pilgrimages to it now see it in its perfection. As beautiful as it is, there is nothing there today which equals a portion of it planned and executed by its owner in the days when her dream garden first began to take shape. On each side of the flagstone steps leading from the lodge down to the creek was a bed of pansies abut a yard wide. In early spring these pansies were a solid mass of blossoms. Walking down the steps between the two beds, this humble onlooker always felt the compulsion to tread softly as though entering some great lecture hall. Upon reaching the foot and turning to face the quaint little blooms, one felt inspired to make a speech, for there was the audience intently gazing up into your face and seeming to say, like Cornelius, **"Now...are we all here present before God, to hear all things that are commanded thee of God" Acts 10:33.**

It is then one concludes the pansy message must be that of *inquisitive thinking,* for they seem to be saying: *"We have followed our Master's will. In obedience to his command we are bearing fruit and making this world a more beautiful place in which to swell by the fragrance of our testimony. But what about you?"*

Thus arrested by their query, with shame one goes back through memory. Looking upon high thoughts noble resolves with which a ladder could be made on which angels might tread, yet upon peering further one finds himself sleeping at the bottom rung. With chagrin comes the admission that high resolves look down upon slumbering acts, failure to utilize opportunities.

Gazing steadfastly into the intelligent faces of these little flowers, there is no thought of explaining failure to give one's best, for they are looking straight into the soul and estimating the flimsiness of such excuses. There then comes from the heart a plea, almost a prayer, for another chance, another opportunity. Then comes the answer with impressive accent, *"Opportunity, oh, the glory of it! Another chance!"*

Another chance! Another day in which to think God's thoughts after him, to ponder upon his way, and then to strive to do his will. Out of the heart, deeply stirred with gratitude is breathed the petition, **"Let the words of my mouth, and the meditation of my heart, be acceptable in thy sight, O Lord, my strength and my redeemer." Psalm 19:14.**

Camellia

The camellia, near of kin to the gardenia, was quite slow in revealing the secrets of its heart. In fact, it was one of the last to, in any measure, speak its mind; and when it did so, it gave no final word but only the expression of a persistent yearning, even as yet unattained.

One afternoon, while walking through one of Norfolk, Va.loveliest gardens, there seemed to be an unspoken but very definite message from the camellia.

It seemed to say: *"My word to the world is not a heart message. It is more of a heart's yearning, and that yearning is for **perfection.** Oh, not that sinless perfection such as some mortals claim. One who boasts of this perfection is perfect in only one thing, and that is folly. I speak of that completion in* *growth which the Master had in mind when he urged his disciples to strive to be perfect just as his Father was perfect, to reach full stature spiritually."*

Such revelation of purpose was calculated to arrest attention. Turning again to this lovely flower, there came the feeling that it had laid its heart bare, and one wondered why she had been so long and so slow in comprehending.

At first glance the camellia seemed just like a very precise and meticulous young lady, costume in perfect taste, cosmetics applied artistically, every tress in place in the modish hair-do. At this look one would say, *"What a perfect flower!"* Yet, drawing nearer, he realized that it failed to attain that for which it so sorely yearned, perfection. It shed no fragrance. It had no odor at all.

What a pity! Just as no person, however painstaking the outward grooming, could reach this goal without the shedding forth of an inner fragrance made by spiritual contact with the Divine, so no flower, regardless of its outward beauty, could ever be considered perfect unless it shared the sweet fragrance of its soul. **"All of you, clothe yourselves with humility toward one another, because, "God opposes the proud but gives grace to the humble." Humble yourselves, therefore, under God's mighty hand, that he may lift you up. 1 Peter 5:5-6.**

The camellia calls to mind the moralist who continually shouts his virtues, all he does or does not do, striving to convince the world of his righteousness. All his morality, charity, respectability, charm only emphasize his one great need, and it seems the Master's words are almost audible, **"One thing thou lackest" Mark 10:21.** Pope once said:

> Whoever thinks a faultless piece to see,
> Thinks what ne'er was,
> Nor is, nor e'er shall be.

So beautiful camellia and admirable moral man, boast

not of perfection. It cannot be found here. Every rose has its thorn. Every day has its night. Even the sun shows spots, and the skies have their darkened clouds.

Still, this is a worthy yearning and a goal which can be ultimately attained when one's hand is placed in the hand of the Omnipotent and one's heart beats in tune with the Divine. This is no mushroom growth but the slow, laborious march of the child of God toward spiritual adulthood. The acorn did not become an oak in a day. The ripened scholar was not made in a single lesson. The trained soldier was not yesterday's raw recruit. Months must pass between seedtime and harvest. Just so, the goal of perfection is attained by slow degrees. It requires the hand of time, but in the end it will be like the shining light which **"shineth more and more unto the perfect day." Proverbs 4:18.**

Until then, the only wise course is to strive continually toward that perfection of which Jesus spoke in his Sermon on the Mount, for the more perfect the soul the more joyous the joys of heaven and the more glorious that glory.

Surely someday, as one walks through the Garden of God (called flowers) in that bright land, he will hear again the voice of the camellia and will be irresistibly drawn to it by its insistent tone. Before near enough to touch it, he will be thrilled by the realization that the yearning of this lovely flower for perfection has been fulfilled, and that this fulfillment exceeds all earthly expectations, for a fragrance beyond compare will fill the celestial air.

Pond Lily

The lily with it message of purity, was chosen to lead the procession of flowers in their Heart Message Pageant. Would it not be fitting to express the pond lily. When a husband passed away, the wife asked God what part of Heaven He (Yeshua) had taken him to and Yeshua responded, *"To the Garden of flowers, where the lilies bloom."* She knew this was so, because the husband had ponds where the lilies bloomed and it gladdened her heart, for she had seen him stand many times meditating near the lily pond.

There is a strong desire to describe its message in personal thought in much the same manner in which the other blossoms have spoken their purpose or yearning. Surely no one could look at the pond lily in its waxen beauty and seeming perfection without the conviction that it has much to tell anyone who will stop for a moment and heed.

However, a poet once recorded a conversation which he had with this lovely piece of excellence and, in its reply to his question, it laid bare its fragrant heart. In so doing it set a standard which all who strive for consecration to the Master and commitment to Christ's service would do well first to ponder and then follow.

Approaching a quiet pool in a shady garden plot, the poet sees the pond lily in its delicate beauty. Transported by the glory of it, he calls out to it in ecstasy:

> O Star on the breast of the river!
> O marvel of human grace!
> Did you fall right down from Heaven,
> Out of the sweetest place?
> You're white as the thoughts of an angel
> Your heart is steeped in the sun;
> Did you grow in the Golden City,
> My pure and radiant one?

However, to this exalted query the pond lily quietly and modestly replies:

> Nay, nay, I fell not out of Heaven
> None gave me my saintly white;
> It slowly grew from the darkness,
> Down in the dreary night.
> From the ooze of the silent river

> I won my glory and grace,
> White souls fall not, O my poet,
> They rise, to the sweetest place.

> Mary Frances Butts

Could here be one who does not yearn, even though it may be secretly, to rise to the highest place? Would you like to do so? The path is marked out plainly to all who will allow the pond lily to point the way. **"Surely goodness and love will follow me all the days of my life, and I will dwell in the house of the LORD forever. Psalm 23:6.**

Resurrection Lily

> A good flower with which to begin is the Resurrection White
> souls fall not, O my poet,
> They rise, to the sweetest place.

> Mary Frances Butts

Lily arrayed in spotless beauty. Its universal message is that of *purity.*

To look upon it in its lovely dress is to remember Jesus' words that **"Solomon in all his glory was not arrayed like one of these." Luke 12:27** To be sure, many commentators claim that the *"lilies of the field"* to which he referred were several varieties of plants, a veritable riot of color. Even so, such lot would still include our stately lily.

Is it not fine that this is our Resurrection flower? How worthy it is of this honor, for it proclaims the matchless purity of the resurrected Lord. **"The LORD rewards every man for his righteousness and faithfulness. 1 Samuel 26:23.**

Not content to stop there, it goes on to speak of the purity that will be ours "when this corruptible shall have put on incorruption, and this mortal shall have put on immortality, then shall be brought to pass the saying that is written, **"Death is swallowed up in victory." 1 Corinthians 15:54.**

Then, indeed, shall we put on a garment more spotless and pure than any lily, no matter how perfect may have been its hue or texture, for we shall be like Him. One time in the Gospel story there is found a glimpse, a foretaste, of this purity that is to be. This is seen on the Mount of Transfiguration.

Some insist that on this mount Jesus drew back the curtain for a moment before his faithful friends, two of whom (Moses and Elijah) had come by way of heaven, three of whom (Peter, James and John) had climbed with him the slopes of this mount and allowed them really to see him at the zenith, the perfection of his humanity. How dazed and amazed were they in the presence of such glory!

Someday, when we who have been converted by grace reach the spiritual adulthood of which he spoke when he said, **"Be ye therefore perfect even as your Father which is in heaven is perfect,"** we will enjoy such glory as was manifested that day, *our purity.* But what of today, this day which the Lord hath made, this day in which we are entreated to rejoice and be glad?

As one looks upon the lovely lily, which delights to magnify the purity of its Creator, there should come an irresistible urge also to bespeak this purity in personal life. Surely this stately flower should stir everyone who looks upon it to breathe this earnest prayer, **"I would be pure, for there are those who trust me."**

Further meditation brings to remembrance the realization that this is the price of admission into the Father's house of many mansions. As David in his Crown Psalm so beautifully posed the question, **"Who shall ascend into the hill of the Lord? And who shall stand in his holy place?"** Then follows the answer, crystal clear, **"He that hath clean hands and a pure heart." Psalm 24:4.**

Passing on to the climax of the appeal of the lily's message, one finds that it is the sure approach to a vision of God. Jesus said, **"Blessed (happy) are the pure in heart; for they shall see God."** The reference here is to more than cleanness; it means wholeness. Its emphasis is upon the undivided heart, the heart which is utterly and absolutely loyal. The beatific vision is only possible here on earth to those with pure hearts. No other can see God now. Sin befogs and clouds the heart so one cannot see him. In the Beatitude purity is used in its widest sense and includes everything. Truly our lovely lily bespeaks such.

Bleeding Heart

Another flower not seen since the days of Grandmother's garden clamors here for the privilege of speaking from its inner self, and its name is the bleeding heart. Do you remember it? Can you not see it there growing in some special spot in an old-fashioned flower plot? Look at it again. See its little head drooped as though it never expected to look up again.

If asked the reason for its dejection or for the meaning of its heart message, it would answer in just the one word, *sacrifice.*

There is a legend concerning this pretty blossom which expresses its thought much clearer than anyone could explain.

On the lower slopes of Calvary, before one ascended to the bare summit which prompted its frequent designation as *"the place of the skull,"* there grew many of the lovely *"lilies of the field,"* and among them was the bleeding heart. However, as tradition goes, in those days it did not droop but stood up stately and erect.

To these flowers it was not unusual to look up and see a man wending his way to Golgotha's crest bearing his own cross. One morning the bleeding heart heard the heavy tramp of feet upon the roadway. Gazing upward, it saw One innately different from any its eyes had ever rested upon.

To be sure, he was carrying his cross and wearing his placard which designated his crime. More than that, pressed down upon his head was a crown of thorns which had cruelly torn his flesh, leaving his forehead caked with blood. Stripped completely, his body bore the marks of an inhuman scourging. Beyond the exhaustion caused by sheer physical torment there seemed to be upon him the weight of all the ills of the world., In spite of all that man had done to abuse and mar his visage, it still was marked indelibly with innocence and purity.

Staring intently into that gentle countenance of goodness, love, and compassion, instinctively the bleeding heart knew that he suffered unjustly, was confident that he was on his way to die for another's guilt. Stunned and overcome by the tragedy of it all, dazed by is own inability to aid in his hour of need to put a stop to this dastardly deed, this tender little flower bowed its tiny head and wept veritable drops of blood.

Unto this day, whenever one looks upon a bleeding heart, he sees its head bent, and from the center of its blossom there emerges what looks to be a drop of blood.

To think upon this little bloom is to send one's thoughts back to Calvary and to make one acutely conscious of the terrible cost, the sacrifice, necessary for our redemption. When one really sees the manner of death he died for us, then he begins to realize what manner of love he had for us.

Sunflower

Perhaps among the loftiest messages breathed by any of the flowers is that of *reverence*, and it is brought by one which never finds itself placed in any formal garden. Possibly this is because it will remain in no set place. No flower bed can hold it, just as no creed nor nation can hold

Him whom every believer reveres. The call is ever, **"Whosoever will, let him come."**

Nor is this large blossom found in the usual flower arrangements, for it will conform to no artistic plan. Wherever it is, it constantly beholds and follows the sun; and when the sunflower sees the sun, it is satisfied.

What a lesson the sunflower pictures to the vast company of professed Christians who are so prone to keep one eye rolled to heaven while the other is set upon the things of earth. Divided loyalty, compromise! How it condemns those who limit the exercise of worship to certain set periods of religious observance on particular days!

Someone has said that there is a little flower in the corner of every heart called reverence which needs watering once a week, and this watering is done by the worship service on the Lord's Day, Sabbath. Surely it would be a great thing for the kingdom of God if every individual professing faith in him would water the blossom of reverence the seventh (Sabbath) day of every week. But why restrict it? Daily worship would make it much more luxuriant.

How can one live, move, breathe one hour of one day without lifting his heart to the Heavenly Father in adoration? The ancient Hebrews were exhorted to remind their children of the ways of the Lord **"when thou sittest in thine house, and when thou walkest by the way, and when thou liest down, and when thou risest up" Deuteronomy 6:7.** When **"thou sittest in thine house,"** think of all the wonders he has provided to make your home beautiful and comfortable: light, radio, TV, phone, heart, things not fully understood by those who, the world says, invented them, but things which the believer understands in the one word reverently whispered, **"GOD."**

"When thou walkest by the way" and become conscious of the fact that **"the heavens declare the glory of God; and the firmament sheweth his handywork." Psalm 19:1.** As one walks his daily path in reverence, he realizes that the sky is God's canopy; the grass, his carpet; the trees, his poetry, and infinitely more beautiful than any poem ever penned by man; the flowers his prose; buildings, boulevards, highways, cars, congregation houses, other things innumerable, all objects of the mind and hand oaf man, but, please God, that mind and hand created an inspired by the Eternal Father.

"When thou liest down," when, after a busy day, the weary body at last rests upon its couch, the face instinctively turns toward the window, the eyes look up and out into the night sky, then the heart again reaches out for a *"Goodnight, Lord Jesus, (Yeshua)."* There is breathed a prayer of thanksgiving for the privilege of sleep as a gracious gift from him. **"He giveth his beloved sleep" Psalm 127:2.** More even than that, there comes a sense of deep gratitude for the certainty that he never sleeps and that his own are in his keeping constantly, in the dark watches of the night as well as in the glorious light of the day.

"When thou risest up." Oh, the glory of the new day! Here is a clean page, a fresh start, bright with the rays of the sun, but brighter still and even more radiant in the sunshine of his love. Facing the wonder of it with all of its promise and opportunity, the reverent soul looks up and whispers;

> Lord, help me to live this day quietly, easily;
> To lean upon thine arm restfully, trustingly;
> to wait for the unfolding of thy will patiently, serenely;
> To meet others peaceably, joyfully
> To face this day courageously, confidently.

Such is the life—plan of the sunflower. It permits no limitation of time or place. It constantly gazes upon the object of its affection, the sun, and follows it from the moment it rises in the East until it sets in the West, drawing daily substance and abounding joy from such reverent worship.

The sunflower by its daily life, seems to be saying to every trusting heart; *"You, too, have a Sun to gaze upon in wonder and admiration, 'the Sun of Righteousness.' Look up! Behold him in all his majesty and beauty. Find the great satisfaction and glory promised to those who thus adore."*

Poppy

The poppy's testimony has become so universally known that should one call for its heart message in any group anywhere, the reply would come in one harmonious chorus, *"Peace."*

Particularly was it vested with this symbol at the close of the First World War, becoming then the Armistice Day flower. Afterward it was given particular honor when Miss Moena Michael of Athens, Georgia, the Poppy Lady, conceived the idea of selling paper poppies on each Armistice Day anniversary. It was she who made the first great anchor of poppies to be cast upon the ocean each November eleventh in memory of the Navy dead of that war. Thereafter, so long as physical strength permitted, Miss Moena went each year to this ceremony. Then, when illness bound her to the wheel chair she continued, even to the end, making the little paper flowers for that design.

Yes, those old enough to remember the thrill of the "cease firing" news which came over the wires that November day in 1918 sum up all the excitement, the gratitude, the prayer and praise of that hour in the one word *"Peace"* and symbolize it with the poppy.

To be sure, the graceful, fragile poppy is sometimes used for another type of peace, a false one; but that is never of its own intention, desire, or volition. All the tragedy following in the train of opium users is but the result of sinful man's distortion of something beautiful, lovable, and God-given.

The poppy stands for a peace which the world knows little of but the kind which it must seek if wars are ever to cease. Myriads of groups or committees or boards of world-wide importance may be appointed. Conference after conference may be held at every strategic point on the globe, but here will never be any lasting peace until the Lord Jesus Christ, **"'The Prince of Peace,"** sits in at such a meeting, yea, even more than that, until he holds the gavel.

The peace which the poppy symbolizes is one which he smiles of the world cannot bestow; nor can the frowns of the world take it away. It is the peace to which every believing soul is rightful heir because Jesus, the blessed Lord, bequeathed it to him. **"The wisdom that comes from heaven is first of all pure; then peace-loving, considerate, submissive, full of mercy and good fruit, impartial and sincere. Peacemakers who sow in peace raise a harvest of righteousness. James 3:17-18.**

Just as an earthly father, seeking worthily to apportion his goods, makes a will for his children, so Jesus, when the time approached for his departure from this world, made his testament. To his Father he commended his spirit; to Joseph of Arimathea, his body, that it might have a decent burial; to the Roman soldiers gambling at the foot of the cross, his raiment; to the beloved disciple, John, his Mother; but what did he leave to his apostles, those faithful believers who had left all to follow him?

Before answering, pause for a moment to recall that in spite of the careless opinion often advanced which assumes that these disciples had nothing to leave when they launched out with him, they really did. Have you regarded the word "fishermen" with disdain? If so, stop, consider, and remember that fishing was one of the leading enterprises of Capernaum. Regardless of his occupation, his station in life, each apostle left his business, him home, his loved ones, his friends, all he held dear from the earthly viewpoint, ALL, to follow Jesus. And following him meant also the taking up of a cross daily!

Verily, verily, in planning his will Jesus would leave

them a good part which could never be taken away; and not only to them but also to every faithful follower of that and every succeeding generation. That is exactly what he did. To them, to you, and to me he bequeathed *his peace.*

Remember how he said there in the upper room, after he had again reminded them of his going away and had urged them not to be troubled of heart: **"Peace I leave with you, my peace I give unto you; not as the world giveth, give I unto you. Let not your heart be troubled, neither let it be afraid." John 14:27.**

That is the peace which the dainty, delicate poppy tries to bespeak. Do you understand it? Have you experienced it in heart and life? If not, would you like to know it? You can. Paul in his beautiful letter to the Philippians sometimes called *"the love letter of the Renewed Covenant"* gives a recipe which never fails (4:5-7). It includes a twofold effort; one set forth from the human standpoint, and the other from the divine.

First, in the giving the human part of this great peace program, Paul says, **"Let your moderation be known unto all men. The Lord is at hand."** Moderation is a poor translation of the Greek word used here., Some use "gentleness" in its place, which is a little better. However, the real meaning is "yielding." **"Let your yielding be made known unto all men. The Lord is at hand."** He is no God so far away that he cannot be touched by our infirmities. He is deeply interested. He is nearer than hand or foot. He is more vital than the air we breathe. You will find that to be true by yielding yourself completely to him, placing all that you are or ever hope to be in adoration at his feet. Submit yourself completely to his will. That is the touchstone of consecration and also the sure avenue to peace.

However, it does not end there. You have only made a beginning of the human side of the peace recipe. Paul continues, **"Be careful for nothing; but in everything by prayer and supplication with thanksgiving let your** requests be made known unto God." Here again there appears a word calling for a better translation. What Paul really said was, **"Don't have anxious, fretful, upsetting care about anything."** Continuing, he directs the Christian disciples to take everything to the throne of grace in prayer and supplication, with thanksgiving.

Often when pondering this blessed passage there come the desire to add to his words about prayer, supplication, and thanksgiving one further admonition: **"And do not give the Lord directions in your prayer."** Few mortals ever present their plea in prayer without adding the manner in which they expect it to be carried out. Then when it is not answered in the manner they expect, they are quite likely to say, *"My prayer was unanswered."*

There is no such thing as an unanswered prayer. God hears and answers every sincere petition. Just as the wise earthly father must at times, for the good of the child, say no, so, many occasions arise in which he who sees the whole plan must say no for the eternal welfare of his own. Yielding to him leads one to trust, though he cannot trace the plan, and to know that someday he will come to see that the Heavenly Father's way was best.

The older one grows, the more he yields his all to the Master, the more he comes to rely upon the third element expressed by Paul in this recipe, "with thanksgiving." Then prayer becomes an expression of complete reliance as he believer reverently thanks God that he who is omniscient, omnipresent and omnipotent knows the perfected plan and does all things well.

Now Paul climaxes his recipe with the divine part of the program: **The peace of God, which passeth all understanding, shall keep your hearts and minds through Christ Jesus."** God's peace which dwells within to strengthen, comfort, and garrison completely, whatever stress and strain may beat upon the soul from without.

Such is the peace of which the poppy speaks. It can be

yours for the asking and receiving. Claim it today.

Daisy

At the mention of the dainty daisy, two thoughts immediately come to mind and apparently they are a paradox. First, everywhere one hears the question continually asked as the graceful petals are plucked from this pretty flower one by one, *"He loves me, he loves me not?"* or *"She loves me, she loves me not?"* Then rapidly upon these queries come the oft-repeated phrase, *"Daisies won't tell."*

Could there be one who has not at some time quizzed the daisy concerning the beloved of the moment? Also, after having received a favorable reply, continued the probe by rubbing the orange center between the palms of the hands then blowing upon the opened palms and counting the particles left to see how many children one would have.

Careful consideration rejects such by-play as the serious message of the daisy to the listening heart. Two very evident aspects cause its discard. Did you ever see one make a cursory estimate of the petals before plying the question, then beginning the quiz in such a way as to receive the desired answer, and following with the "children" part, give an extra whiff at the palms to make certain it, too, would prove favorable? It has been done thus, and surely the daisy from its gracious heart would be a party to no such deception.

However, done with the strictest scruples, this plan could never express the daisy's real thoughts. Tearing a lovely flower apart willfully is cruel. It smacks too much of a third degree. No one wants ruthlessly to wrest the daisy's message from it. This must be spontaneous and free.

"Daisies won't tell" come nearer expressing his dainty flower's heart. Growing in a large open field or by the roadside, blown gently to and fro by a summer's breeze, it is as stately and queenly as though growing in some formal garden. It seems to have an inner sufficiency and satisfaction

the world knows not and its word to the inquire is that of *reserve*.

Looking upon the daisy wherever it is found growing, in attractive or unattractive surroundings, drawn by its grace and daintiness, yet feeling unquestionably its stateliness and stamina, there comes a striking comparison. In its quiet withdrawal from that which would warm, in its reserve it calls to mind the believer who is in this world but is not of this world.

The green of its leaves and stem reminds the Christian that he is a new creature in Christ Jesus. The white of its petals speaks of the purity to be sought by him who is hidden in the righteousness of God and who should strive to lift to the Father clean hands and a pure heart. The gold of its center tells of the reward to be enjoyed when the child of faith reaches spiritual adulthood and the glory to be experienced when he actually takes possession of his heavenly citizenship.

Contemplation of such exalted position and the joy it affords calls keenly to mind the fact that the believer is a pilgrim here, tarrying but at night. He is in the world as an ambassador of Christ, to tell the good news of salvation, to help the sick, comfort the sorrowing, feed the hungry, and minister in every possible way in the dear Saviour's name. Walking in this sin-sick world, he often finds himself soiled and defiled by its mark, and he must constantly turn to the Master for cleansing and healing.

Still, the Believer is not of this world. He is clothes in Christ, in his righteousness, just as the daisy is wrapped in its reserve; and regardless of outward circumstances, both are the recipients of an inner glory, the half of which has never been told.

Tube Rose

Another rose has revealed its little heart, the tube rose,

and is message is the of *sorrow*. One wonders whence its name, for there seems to be nothing about it which would like it to the rose family. As is often the case in human life, it seems alien to its group, standing ever aloof and alone.

Could it be that herein lies a part of its message? Sorrow has no rightful place in the family of the perfected kingdom. It was God's will that man live in continual fellowship with him. Sin came, taking its toll and leaving sorrow in its wake.

Pondering the message of this tiny flower has brought serious self-searching. The thought recurs. Does the tube rose really speak of sorrow, or has its word come from an association of ideas? So many things linger in the memory in that way. One hears a strain of music, and it's always open up the same train of thought.

Just so, there comes but a whiff of its heavy odor and immediately there is called to remembrance a beloved uncle, who, whenever possible, wore a tube rose in his lapel. How pretty it looked in his buttonhole, and what a fragrance it exuded! How much a part of the perfection surrounding him in the eyes of an adoring niece! Then suddenly, in the height of young manhood, he slipped away after so brief an illness that it left loved ones staggered by the blow. Uncle Harvey was gone. Uncle Harvey, tube roses, sorrow! The three forever linked in a young woman's heart.

Still, this heart message is something deeper than an association in an individual mind. The tube rose seems to say that when touched by the compassion of the divine, even the dark experiences can be made pure and white, shedding abroad in the life a deep fragrance of heavenly origin.

It seems to remind one that from such suffering have emerged some of the strongest souls. Many of the world's greatest characters are marked with terrible scars, and often through their tears have the sorrowful first seen the gates of heaven. There could be no rainbow in the heart were there no tears in the eyes. Someone has said:

> Alas! By some degree of woe
> We every bliss must gain;
> The heart can ne'er a transport know
> That never feels a pain

George Lyttelton

As the fragrant, delicate tube rose points out the pathway of sorrow, it seems to be calling attention to the truth that this path and this alone, this one trod before us by the God-man, Yeshua, often referred to as the Man of Sorrows, leads to the land where sorrow is unknown.

No one has ever reached that celestial abode without finding thorns in his path. However, if each could call back a word to those left behind, surely he would insist that the very memory of sorrow is a benediction and that in its every burden is found a blessing.

Forget-Me-Not

To a tiny flower, so small that it is often passed by unnoticed, so unpretentious that even its name is a plea for attention, comes the privilege of delivering a testimony of great import, for the forget-me-not speaks the heart message of *constancy*.

Someone has aptly said that constancy is the complement of all other human virtues, for without it there is neither love nor friendship nor even virtue itself in the world.

Shakespeare said, "O Heaven! Were man but constant, he were perfect."

Could it be, that as the Heavenly Father looks down upon his congregation, pondering his plans for it, grieving over human failure to reach the divine possibilities, he, too, is heard to sigh: *"O Heaven! Were Christians, those redeemed by the blood of my only begotten Son, those called by my name, but constant, they would reach the completion planned for them, the spiritual adulthood of which my Son spoke when he said, 'Be ye therefore perfect, even as your Father which is in heaven is perfect'"* **Matthew 5:48**.

Believers are so likely to blow hot and cold. One day, moved by some sermon, lesson, anthem, or experience to the heights of zeal, and in response to such an urge the Christian makes some outward commitment. Then in time the fervor cools. The loyalty becomes spasmodic. Outside things creep ink, and all too soon the life which could have meant much in kingdom values becomes actually detrimental to the Master's cause. Someone has said that many resolves are born but too often they are stillborn.

This business of being a Christian is a constant affair. It requires every bit of one, every moment of the day, every day of the year. One glibly quotes, **"This is the day which the Lord hath made; we will rejoice and be glad in it." Psalm 118:24**, then mentally pigeonholes this lovely verse in the Sunday file. Who said the psalmist thought only of the Sabbath day or of some particular religious day of the Israelites? Every day is the Lord's day. Every day is the time in which to rejoice and be glad in consecration and joyful service. Every day is the time to be constant and faithful to the Master, even to the point of taking up the cross in order to follow worthily. Those who in trust call upon the name of the Lord Jesus, who have accepted his salvation by grace through faith, are enlisted in his service for live, for every day of life. Today, believers live eternally.

The forget-me-not is little, inconspicuous, easily trampled upon, has no favored place in the garden, yet it is satisfied and content. It finds such serenity in the knowledge that it is in God's keeping and care. It knows that the God of all creation is its Creator, too. It is assured that, regardless of its size, place or position, from the earthy standpoint, will never forsake it, and having such confidence, it find its joy in endless devotion.

Chrysanthemum

The fall season, considered by some as sad and dying, is really a time of fruition and glory. It produces a radiant flower which spreads abroad the message of *cheerfulness,* the chrysanthemum. There it is at every turn of the way singing its gladsome song, *"Be of good cheer."* It is like a summer day shedding its brightness all around.

Any attempt to characterize its loveliness would be to say that it is of a patrician type for not only is it graceful and beautiful but it also seems to have dignity and brains. It manifests wondrous strength and lasting power. Its spirit is all sunshine. Its grace springs from gladness. It is beautiful because it is bright. Its cheerfulness exudes health. It has real stamina in its being.

Unlike its companion flower of the season, the dahlia, the charming "mum" never flaunts itself.

Probably it would be well to hesitate for a moment before continuing with its heart message to contrast there two flowers. When doing so, an experience is always brought vividly to mind.

It was an occasion when there was the privilege of speaking about the flowers at a lovely banquet. The tables were arranged with colorful and attractive flower motifs, the most imposing one, of course, being at the head table. Absorbed with the thing to be done and weighed down by the responsibility of an important part on the program, there was little time to consider these flowers other than the subconscious note of the charm of each piece as a unit. Upon the conclusion of the address, imagine the personal embarrassment when the toastmaster turned and said, *"Even though you were severe with the dahlias, we want you to have this bowl of them."*

Surely everyone agrees the dahlias are beautiful, but their beauty seems so superficial. They are conceited, and a little brazen in this conceit. They call to mind the Scripture, **"Pride goeth before destruction and an haughty spirit before a fall." Proverbs 16:18,** for they flaunt themselves today and tomorrow fade. They remind one of proud, pompous people who are all "front door," with no stamina, no inner radiance, beautiful, indeed, but without heart interest in the world need.

Not so, the cheerful chrysanthemum. It seems to be urging one to look for the sunlight which God sends into every day. It reminds those who look upon it that God is glorified, not by groans but by thanksgivings, as it puts the heart in tune to sing his praises. It seems to urge one to **"rejoice in the Lord always." Philippians 4:4.**

By its note of cheer its lightens poverty, affliction, and illness, reminding the troubled that every path will be more easily traveled, every load will be less burdensome, and every shadow will lift sooner if approached in the joyful spirit of the redeemed.

It calls to remembrance the adage that *"every cloud has a silver lining"* and urges its friends to look for the brighter side. Surely it must add the admonition to continue to gaze upon its inner radiance rather than the gray exterior.

The chrysanthemum must sing as it works. One can almost hear its glad refrain. Even through the year is not at the spring and the day is not at the morn, the theme is still that of Pippa's song:

> God's in his heaven -
> All's right with the world.

Cosmos

The next flower to lay bare its heart is the cosmos, and it speaks of *aspiration.* Why? Because the dainty, graceful cosmos seems forever to have its pretty head in the clouds. With a gracious nod it seems to rise above its surroundings, surroundings which may be either a well-ordered garden or one full of weeds, into the spiritual world of higher things

It seems to be saying to everything and everybody,

"Heads up! Eyes to the skies! You are made for something far better." It reminds the believer that, though he is in the world (and oftentimes he surroundings here are not pleasant not conducive to spiritual growth), he is not of the world. His citizenship is in heaven. He should mind heavenly things.

Surely there is never a heart which has not had or does not have its moments of longing, yearning for something better, higher, nobler, holier than it has ever known. Unless here is something which one prefers above the physical life their physical life will become tiresome, useless, bore some, and empty.

The gospel of Jesus Christ supplies this something. It is the vey fruit of aspiration. The gospel, the good news of the saving grace of our blessed Lord, is to the heart what spring is to the earth. Just as spring makes every root, blade, and bud stir and desire to be something more, just so the glad tidings if allowed entrance, move within the heart.

The gospel awakens new thoughts, impulses, and desires. It moves on with a new motive. It sets one's soul toward a higher goal and makes him want to forget those things which are behind and reach forth **"unto those things which are before"** as he presses **"toward the mark for the prize of the high calling of God in Christ Jesus." Philippians 3:12-14.**

So, with a toss of its dainty head and a smile on its pretty face which bespeaks the assurance that it has learned the lesson of true aspiration, the lovely cosmos seems to be saying,

> Come up higher, come up higher,
> From the lowlands and the mire.

Then the heart truly reached by the gospel message realizes how vain are the things of earth, no matter how well-ordered they may have seemed. It comes also to say that one can rise above and overcome even the weeds of discouragement, disappointment, of disease and doubt. Thus cleansed and consecrated by such meditation, this heart lifts up its voice to the Master and in prayer pleads:

> Lord, lift me up and let me stand,
> By faith, on heaven's tableland.
> A higher plane than I have found;
> Lord, plant my feet on higher ground.
>
> Johnson Oatman, Jr.

Gladiola

A chance remark one day unlocked he true message of the gladiola. Someone had sent my Mother a box of exquisite assorted flowers, among which were several stalks of gladioli and a box of Whitman's Chocolate Candy. While arranging them she said, *"I always put gladioli in a vase first, for I have found they are always going to do their own way."*

"Always going to do their own way," whatever that way might be at the moment. Stated a bit differently, *temperamental.* Yes, that is the message of the many-colored gladiola.

"Temperamental" expresses the atmosphere of character, and generally that expression is an insistence upon one's own way. To be sure, that way may produce a beautiful result. Slipping back through memory lane, here is no remembrance of "glads" ever looking other than lovely in any flower arrangement, and following closely upon that thought comes the query, why shouldn't they, if they had the choice of position and other flowers, just as attractive, had to accept the places left?

How like some people they are! Should one go further and say, How like some Christians they are! Believers, capable, talented, useful in the glorious Kingdom work, whose service is contingent upon their being allowed choice of time, place, and subject! Believers who are competent to achieve admirable results demanding to be handled with kid gloves, much of the beauty of their service being lost because they are temperamental. **"Trust in the LORD with all your heart and lean not on your own understanding; in all your ways acknowledge him, and he will make your paths straight. Proverbs 3:5-6.**

In the hands of the skilled horticulturist this temperamental quirk of the gladiola is ignored and he places the stately bloom in the position of his choice, the result being beautiful beyond expression. Is not the same true of the life placed completely in the hands of the divine Florist?

Someone has said that if religion does nothing for our temper, it has done nothing for our soul. One might go further and say that if it has done nothing for our temperament, it has done nothing for our soul. However successful may seem the outward results, when one has insisted upon his way, unmindful of the desires or best interests of others, he can in no wise reach the heights of beauty and holiness planned for his life had it been completely surrendered to God's plan, ready to fit into his way, whatever that might be.

Jesus, in stating his mission, said that he came not to do his own will (way) but the will of the Father who sent him. Can flower or man afford to change this pattern laid down by the Master?

Carnation

Probably no flower has been more generous with its message than the carnation. Who can number the sick, the sorrowing, the lonely of heart who have received strength from its word of *courage;* for courage is the thought emanating from its lovely heart and pervading the very air it breathes.

There are two particular human experiences in which its ministry is a blessing. One is the sick room. The carnation is the ideal flower there. It endures so well, standing erect, proud, and fragrant for days. To the suffering one it says, **"Only be thou strong and very courageous." Joshua 1:7.** In some mysterious way it seems to transmit its courage to the ailing one, giving a vital boost in an hour when it is most needed.

The carnation can cheer the heart both night and day! How often they radiate their God-given message to stimulate in the fight for health! Even today their word can still be heard: **"Be strong and of good courage." Joshua 1:6.** All things are not good. Ah, no! But **"All things work together for good to them that love God, to them who are the called according to his purpose." Romans 8:28.**

Looking back through the span of a few brief years, one sees confirmed in personal experience, not only the heart message of the beautiful carnation, but also the deep, abiding truth of these words from the pen of the beloved apostle Paul.

No, all things are not good. It is distressing to be laid aside when there is so much to be done in the Master's service and so much one wants to do, to say nothing of the discomfort of actual physical suffering. However, they do *"work together for good"*, those trying, unpleasant, lonely, painful experiences. Through communion with the blessed Lord, one soon finds his couch to be verdant, that he has been made to lie down in pastures green. He comes to see that this period of waiting is but a season of preparation for some larger field. It brought a new personal appreciation of the Book of books, giving time for earnest meditation upon his Word and sending the writer forth to teach the unsearchable riches of this treasury of truth.

In the hour of suffering the brave carnation also reminds the faithful that God will not allow one to be tried more than he is able to bear. It is possible that the illness, found so troublesome, is but the privilege of having fellowship with him in his suffering. Paul prayed that he might have **"the fellowship of his sufferings" Philippians 3:10.** Peter admonished believers to rejoice **"inasmuch as ye are partakers of Christ's suffering." 1 Peter 4:13.** And when Paul assured believers that **"if we suffer, we shall also reign with him" 2 Timothy 2:12.**

Thus to the weary heart, harassed by physical incapacity, comes joy, comfort, survival, and hope as, through the eyes of faith, dawns the realization that out of this experience will come something sweeter and finer and better than he has ever imagined. The dauntless courage of this fine flower floods his being. With the return of health and strength come a new light to the eye, a song in the heart, the spirit of a victor. Through the power of the Creator of the carnation, his own Creator, more than that, his Redeemer and Lord, he goes forth conquering and to conquer in the name of him who said, **"Be of good cheer; I have overcome the world." John 16:33.**

Again, the stalwart carnation brings its message of courage when death has left its solemn hush. It breathes forth Jesus' strength-giving words, **"Let not your heart be troubled, neither let it be afraid" John 14:27.**

Remember! All the sting, hurt, bafflement, loneliness, and heartache of death is of sin and the devil. It is experienced only by the bereaved. The believer walks *"through the valley of the shadow of death"* unafraid because he is not alone. In the word "valley" comes the picture of something lonely and possibly dark, yet robbed of its cheerlessness by him who said, **"I am the light of the world" John 8:12.** But what about the shadow in the valley? This valley is an actual valley which David led his sheep through.

Shadows can do no harm. Did the shadow of a pistol ever blast a brain or the shadow of a sword ever cleave a head? Then how can the shadow of death really inflict lasting harm? Physical death is but a shadow, appearing in somber garb, to be sure, but robbed of its power by him against whom the gates of death and hell cannot stand. Spiritual death, separation from God eternally, holds no terror for the Christian because of his oneness with Christ. To him physical death is but passing through an open door, going home.

One is so prone to forget these things. The carnation says: **"Don't be bewildered and afraid. Where is your courage? Remember how He said, 'I am he that liveth, and was dead; and behold, I am alive for evermore, Amen; and have the keys of hell and of death'" Revelation 1:18.**

In answer, the believer lifts his eyes and heart in faith while, in the words of the Father, replying:

> No haunting dread of Death,
> My mind is all at ease;
> After my latest breath
> I know who hold the Keys.
>
> --
>
> No frantic fear of Hell,
> My soul no terror sees;
> Assured all will be will
> I know who hold the Keys.

Marigold

The next flower bidding for attention is a relative of the carnation, its cousin, in fact, the marigold, and its heart message is *obedience.*

What a lesson its testimony is to the believer! Even those born anew in Christ Jesus, a part of his great body (the congregation) are often apt to become jealous and dissatisfied or else to become excuse-makers in an attempt to avoid effort and labor in his vineyard.

No doubt you have heard someone, perhaps yourself, make remarks like the following:

"If I could only speak as So-and So does, I would be delighted to take an assignment at any time."

"If I could sing, I would be...."
"What's-his-name is so talented. If I just had a talent for something...."
"Mrs. Thing-a-ma-jig is so pretty. People are satisfied just to look at her. If I...."

Thus one might continue indefinitely, but then you are familiar with each and every such excuse.

How easy it would be for the marigold to say: *I am not fragrant like my lovely Cousin Carnation. In fact, my odor is even offensive to some. I wear not her delicate hues. There are those who do not think me pretty at all. I am never featured in a beautiful bud vase. No one ever lets me be used in profusion at a wedding. There is no need of my trying to be anything."*

That sounds as if it might be some human speaking, does it not? Wanting the *"chief place in the synagogue"* but not willing to pay the price of advancement! Continually forgetting that there are other avenues of service than those in the forefront. Never stopping to consider that there are many tasks, not so pleasant, which must be done to complete the Kingdom pattern. Ignoring the truth that to everyone is given some fruit-bearing talent in his glorious service. Refusing to go apart with God in communion and there find what it is he wishes done and how one should do it, then consecrating all to him in obedience however small the task may seen from the standpoint of the world.

Not such philosophy does one find in the obedient marigold. Far different in its message to the waiting world. Falling back into almost the exact words of its Maker, it states: **"My meat is to do the will of my Father and to finish his work. It is not for me to question place or prominence. It is but for me to obey, so I will follow the will of my Maker. I will be fruitful."** Then, in accordance with this resolve, it blooms and blooms, and its blossoms last in obedience to his will.

The marigold is a good steward. Do you remember the standard for one? Paul said, **"Moreover it is required in stewards that a man be found faithful" 1 Corinthians 4:2.** Jesus, in referring to a faithful servant, said, **"Blessed is that servant, whom his Lord when he cometh shall find so doing" Luke 12:43.**

Surely the obedient marigold meets every requirement of faithfulness and merits the commendation of the Lord, **"Well done, thou good and faithful servant:....enter thou into they joy of the Lord: Matthew 25:21.**

Brown-Eyed Susan

This little manuscript had been completed. In fact, there has been a hurried typing of the material. It was then awaiting a more careful copying in which there would be an earnest effort to eliminate the many errors which arose thruough the faulty "hunt and peck" system of writing.

Just as this moment came the opportunity and privilege of a much-longed-for week end on the beautiful beach of Virginia. Since the destination, an attractive little cottage, was reached after dark, there was little chance to glory in the grandeur of the place that first evening; the moonlight on the ocean was beautiful; but after an early breakfast the following morning, we all set out to enjoy as much as possible of the gorgeous panorama which stretched out all about this lovely site.

The most interesting drive of the day was down the highway and into the sandy hills of Nags Head, North Carolina. If you have ever had the privilege of this unforgettable ride, you will remember how the road rides straight down the ocean front, where the first flight (plane) of the Wright Brothers took place.

Indelibly imprinted upon the mind is the picture meeting the eye at the first turn of the road. There stood a clump of the largest brown-eyed Susan's imaginable. They seemed to be wearing unusually bright yellow dresses, and their large brown eyes bespoke their cordial welcome. Each one seemed to be saying, *"Hello. We are so glad you came!"* At each turn there would be a fresh group of these cheery flowers, looking just as though they had been appointed to the entertainment committee and were waiting there to wave their friendly greeting. Then upon reaching the destination, sand after sandy hill of them, truly a riot of glorious yellow, joined the others in their note of welcome. Praise whomever planted them.

It was clearly evident that if one felt strange in this community, it would be through no fault of the brown-eyed Susan, for it seemed eager to make its offer of friendship to all who would stop to give ear. Its gracious spirit seemed to fill the air and to lead one to the realization of its heart message, that of *friendliness*. I desire to be more like this kind of friend:

F - Fun-loving; faithful
R – Risk being real, even misunderstood
I – Interested in the welfare of others
E - Expect the best of others: Empathetic
N – Natural relationship; Non-exclusive
D – Diplomatic; Delightful; Durable
S – Sympathetic; Supportive; Stable
H – Helpful; Hopeful; Happy
I – Interdependent by helping others
P – Patient; Protective of confidences; Personable

Surely everyone in our party felt refreshed and glad in the presence of these gay little flower people, felt a new thrill of happiness at the privilege of being there, and felt a deep sense of gratitude for the friendliness these golden blossoms extended. The bees were thoroughly enjoying them.

Someone has said that everyone should look for the sunlight which the Father sends into our days. Indeed God send his sunshine that day in the form of these pretty brown-eyed Susans, for they seemed like a sunny day, shedding their brightness all around. The light on their friendly little faces communicated the happy spirit which inspired it.

Their friendliness made the brown-eyed Susan's merit a central place in memory's portrait of a day that will not soon be forgotten, for they made every effort to help a humble visitor feel cordially welcome and a vital part of it all.

To the mind came this query. How many are there today who are turning sharp, unexpected and oftimes frightening turns on life's highways to whom a friendly nod or word of greeting might not only be welcome but, more than that, also be desperately needed?

Continuing along this mental avenue, the thoughts are confronted with a sad feeling of failure time and time and again in making this much-needed offer. To be sure, there are few who intentionally withhold friendliness, but in the hurry and bustle of the day one is likely to become so absorbed in the things of self, however important they may be, that he fails to be sensitive to the needs of those he meets along the way. He should remember that, regardless of the plaudits of the world for accomplishments, he has lost the art of living if he has ceased to offer his hand in friendly clasp.

The cheerful brown-eyed Susan with its generous offer of friendliness makes one who has caught its message stop for serious self-examination. It reminds him that he who puts one touch of sunshine into the life of any man, woman, or child has achieved much in heaven's sight, for he has become a laborer together with God.

Aster

Another relative of the carnation is the aster. Its kinship seems even closer than that of the marigold. Possibly one would call it a first cousin. Not so much because it, too, is dainty, graceful, and delicate in hue, but more because of the closer relationship of their heart message. The dainty aster speaks to the listening ear the note of *patience.* Surely patience is so like fortitude (courage) that it seems almost a sister or daughter.

It has been said that patience is the key to contentment. A glance at the affable aster discloses the fact that it has found this to be true, and it pleads for all who will heed to find this satisfaction of soul.

Bending nearer and listening intently, one will hear the aster explain further that patient waiting is often the highest way of doing God's will, that sometimes he asks nothing of his children except silence, patience, and maybe tears. However, even in this there is power. One is reminded that, with time and patience, the mulberry leaf becomes silk.

David expressed the aster's message in another form when he said, **"Wait on the Lord" Psalm 37:34.** Certainly both would urge one to hold on, hold fast, hold out, ever remembering that this quality of patience is not passive but active, that it is concentrated strength. It fortifies the spirit, sweetens the temper, stifles anger, extinguishes envy, subdues pride, bridles the tongue, restrains the hand, and tramples upon temptation.

To be sure, someone will come forth with admonition to remember that patience is sometimes bitter, but even to that can be added the certainty that her fruit is sweet. Again one is reminded that all things are not good, but they do work together for good to them who love God, them who are chosen according to his purpose.

So the gentle aster would assuredly affirm that never for a moment should one consider God's delays his denials. Even in them one lives his role in the sphere of the great Kingdom work, for **"they also serve who only stand and wait."** There is no music in a rest, but there is the making of music in it. So many people are continually missing that part of life's melody, always talking of perseverance, courage, and fortitude, unmindful of the fact that patience is the finest, worthiest, rarest part of fortitude.

So, with its last breath the graceful aster will continue to plead with any who will hear, urging him to listen to the words of the Lord as recorded by the psalmist, **"Be still, and know that I am God" Psalm 46:10.** Certainly its final word to the believing heart would be: *"Trust God to weave your thread into the great Web even though the pattern does not yet show."*

Petunia

It has been said that happiness is a fragile thing. How true! One awakens on a bright sunny morning with a song in the heart. Not only is there sunshine without but also it seems to penetrate the innermost being. Breakfast is usually appetizing, the family cheerful; there are prospects of a fine day as its tasks are assumed either in the business realm or about the home duties. Anticipating the work and play of the day, one is about to conclude that this is really a good old world after all.

Then crash! Bang! Into the pattern so pleasing but a moment before something unexpected intrudes. Maybe a word carelessly spoken, a thought unbidden, something of so little consequence that, in later contemplation it is actually hard to point out. However, with its appearance all the brightness of the day is enveloped in gloom.

How truly the petunia, which speaks the message of *happiness,* depicts such an experience! Look at it growing in the flower bed or box, surrounded by the other members of its family, each one decked out in some bright, gay color. It is so happy that it seems to toss its tiny head for sheer joy. Surely it must be pondering the thrill of living.

Then a hand reaches forth, plucks it from its natural habitat and places it in some man-made flower arrangement. In no time at all the fact is plainly evident that for the petunia the joy of the day is gone, and soon it hangs its little head in sorrow for its lost happiness.

It finds its greatest joy in union with its Creator, in serving where he placed it. Its strength and happiness consist in glorifying God there. It finds bliss, not in seeking some formal show but in forgetting self in the wondrous joy of service, in living its little life at its best in God's chosen spot. To be happy is not the purpose of its being, but to live life at its best and in that way to deserve happiness.

It seems to say to all who will hear that true happiness is the natural fruitage of love which expresses itself in devoted service to the Master. It reminds one that such can never come by making it an end. Those who seek it directly find much heartache and sorrow in the path. By seeking to glorify God in loving ministry, it is attained.

The petunia, a fragile thing, nodding and swaying in the gentle breeze, seems to say, "O foolish man! Do not look for happiness in the distance. Be wise and find it growing at your feet."

Happiness is a born twin. If one would gain such joy, he must share it. The petunia shares its beauty and bliss of being with all who will receive. As it blooms and blesses where ever its seed is dropped, whether in humble garden plot or in a stately formal bed, it bursts forth in all its glory, reminding one that not in place or condition but in the mind alone can one be made happy or miserable.

The heart beating in unison with the heart of God, tuned to his will and purposes, finds expression in loving service which gives such happiness as the world can never know.

Nasturtium

From almost the inception of this little "Garden of the Heart" there was ever present the desire to have the nasturtium find its place therein. Time after time it was approached with a plea for its message. Each time it was gay and smiling and pleasing but also mum. Finally, in desperation, there escaped the exclamation, *"You are just as queer as you can be!"*

However, quickly upon this cry came the thought, *"Not queer, oh, no! Such a dispenser of good cheer could never be considered queer."* Seeking to explain it, there first came the word *"different";* but it did not satisfy. Then in quick succession followed the thought *"individual";* and in the utterance of this term *individual* came the revelation of the nasturtium's heart message.

Certainly a thing so generous and joyous in the spreading of happiness could never be called queer. Still, one cannot fail to note the fact that information, texture, odor, and even coloring it seems to stand alone. It is individual.

Could it be that therein lies its charm? Someone has said that each individual nature has its own beauty. Surely from its individuality springs the nasturtium's true beauty.

It is satisfied merely to be itself. It never seeks to copy the hue or texture of another blossom. It is truly free because it is sufficient unto itself. It seems to believe that in God's plan it has a particular place, a special mission in being itself at its best.

Looking upon it in its fruitfulness and its seeming thrill in service, one is led to self-contemplation. There comes the serious query, What is there in me which, if brought to its best in expression, could be well used in the ongoing of God's kingdom? There is no NO-talent person in the Master's program. Each has his unique place to fill. Have you as an individual found yours? Have you earnestly sought it? If not, now is the time to do so. Dare to be different, individual, for him.

Probably it is well to be reminded that not in armies nor in nations have the races advanced, but here and there in the course of the ages an individual has stood up and cast his shadow over the entire world. Could it be that today the Saviour is waiting for you to stand up, to step out, alone, for him and his cause? Could it be that your individuality at its best, consecrated to him, is what this sin-sick world needs just now to kindle the fire of great revival?

The nasturtium blesses wherever it touches simply by being itself, individual. If this old world is ever conquered for Christ, it will be by each one doing his own work, filling his own sphere, holding his own part, and saying to the blessed Jesus, **"Lord, what wilt thou have me do?"**

Blue Delphinium

While discussing flowers one evening with a lovely friend, more than eighty summers young, she ventured the hope that her favorite flower grew in this little "Garden of the Heart." Upon inquiry, her blossom proved to be the blue delphinium. No other color would suffice, just the blue one.

Again and again during this brief visit the conversation would be intentionally steered back to this pretty bloom in an effort to learn if its charm lay in some particular message revealed to its admirer's heart. The reply would always be the same: *"It does not say anything especially to me, but I think it is the most beautiful flower that grows."*

Long after the evening had passed, the blue delphinium clamored for attention. Continually it was broached with the question, *"What are you trying to say? What is your heart message?"*

Finally it answered, breathing its theme on definitely that one wondered why the delay in hearing it. While peeking in with the mind's eye upon an imaginary bed of blue delphinium in full bloom, the words of the poet, that *"heaven is a fair blue stretch of sky,"* came vividly to consciousness, and with this sentence came the realization that these gracious, graceful flowers were trying to speak of heaven, if one would listen. Surely their love of heaven had made them heavenly in beauty, texture, and color.

The difficulty which face the blue delphinium is transmitting its heart message but reminds that one of the hardest lessons to learn in this life, and one which some seem never to learn is to see the divine, the celestial, in simple, familiar things near at hand, to realize that heaven lies about us here in this world.

A bed of these delicate blooms, a veritable sea of blue, perfectly mirrors the visible heavens. More than that, it sets the devout heart to dreaming of that perfect House of many mansions in which, by God's grace, some day we will abide. Heaven.

What dreams, hopes, aspirations the word awakens! *Heaven,* the day of which grace is the dawn. *Heaven,* the ripe fruit of which grace is the blossom. *Heaven,* the glorious home to which grace is the pathway. *Heaven,* the joy, peace, and comfort of which there is a foretaste on earth, the glory and fulfillment of which awaits in the Better Land.

Looking again at heaven reflected in this beautiful expanse of blue, each blossom in the bed seemed to be saying that the unseen heaven, too, is made up of flowers; for all the saints up there are flowers in the Garden of God, and their holy love is the fragrance which they send out to fill the bowers of paradise.

Returning again and again to the bed of blue delphinium, so perfect and exquisite, surely all will agree with the poet who said:

> If God hath made this world so fair,
> Where sin and death abound,
> How beautiful beyond compare,
> Will Paradise be found!

Montgomery

Violet

For some reason the thought of pansies always suggests one of its near of kin, the violet. They are so closely related in appearance and spirit, quiet and modest, yet mammoth in the joy and inspiration they bring. While the pansy urges one to meditation and intelligent consideration, its little friend, the violet, speaks of the conclusion which comes to every thoughtful heart which has reverently dwelt upon the deep things of God, the message of *humility.*

Generally the word *"humility"* brings to the mind the thought of being little, modest, unassuming, meek, all of which might well be used to describe the violet. However, the last adjective, in its fullest sense, gives the best description of the heart message of this dainty little flower. Its fragrance speaks of the fragrance of meekness. To think of these shy little blossoms is to remember the words of the beloved Master when he said, **"Blessed are the meek: for they shall inherit the earth." Matthew 5:5.**

Meekness is the gentleness of strength. It is spiritual poise and strength. Though misuse has sometimes coupled it with weakness, there is no foundation for such a designation. There is nothing weak in meekness. The English word has been allowed to stray from its original meaning. Go back to God's Word and analyze it there.

The Bible records, **"The man Moses was very meek." Numbers 12:3.** Surely there could never be found one who would dare to accuse of weakness the man who stood fearlessly before Pharaoh, who gallantly led his people through a dry path miraculously made in the Red Sea, who in obedience to God's command struck the rock and brought forth a refreshing stream to his famished followers; who talked with God on Mount Sinai, and who in the face of the grievous sin of his people pleaded that his own name be blotted out of the book of life for their transgressions that they might live.

Again, in the Renewed Testament, hear the blessed Saviour say of himself, **"I am meek and lowly in heart." Matthew 11:29.** Most assuredly there is nothing weak about Jesus. So many pictures, seeking to depict him, fail completely to grasp and portray the quiet, masterful strength on that gentle, peaceful countenance. One marked by weakness could never have authoritatively commanded the boisterous sea to **"Be still!** Nor would a weakling ever have dared to call the organized religionists of the day **"hypocrites,...blind...guides,...serpents,...generation of vipers." Matthew 23.**

Look then, more closely for a true picture of the meek. What characterizes them? The meek quietly submit to God and his Word. They joyfully comply with his design. They are gentle toward all men. They are willing to bear provocation without being inflamed by it. They are silent or else return a soft answer. They show displeasure whenever the occasion demands, without indulging in any indecencies. They prefer to forgive twenty injuries rather than to strive to avenge one. One has but to listen to find that the humble little violet is seeking to portray just such a message.

Returning to the Beatitude for further description of the meek, one reads that **"they shall inherit the earth."** This also our modest little violet does. It even dresses for the role of this inheritance, for it wears the royal color, purple. It looks like a sovereign. It does not take up much of the earth, but it has enough, all it needs.

In like manner, someday when the believer has finished his earthly pilgrimage and entered the house of many mansions, he will wear the robe of immortal royalty. He will then receive, not only an incorruptible crown, but also his inheritance in the heavenly Canaan where today his citizenship is registered. Thus, all the blessedness of heaven above and earth beneath becomes the portion of the meek.

So, dear, lovely, modest, little violet, in your gentleness, your humility, your quiet strength, and your meekness you make a splendid pattern which every believer should seek to emulate, and in the opinion of this humble writer you are the most precious flower that grows.

Violets, a shy violets!

How many hearts with thee compare,
who hide themselves in thickest green,
and thence unseen
Ravish the unraptured air
With sweetness, dewy, fresh and rare!
--
Violets, shy violets!
Human hearts to me shall be
Viewless violets in the grass,
And as I pass,
Odor and sweet imagery
Will wait on mine and gladden me.

George Meredith

The violet loves a sunny bank,
the cowslip loves the lea,
the scarlet creeper loves the elm;
But I love, Thee.

Orchid

    This beautiful flower continues forward, gathering strength to carry on, reaching goals, aiming for the stars and not giving up. It has healing properties which with each step you take, you are drawn closer and closer to the Master. Continue reaching for the stars and always focus on the perfect outcome of Heaven. There is no need to accept anything less than the love of our Saviour.

    I am going to list many other flowers that you may desire to research and discover their messages for each one has its own central message of the heart. Let the flower speak directly to you and touch them, each has its own feel and energy. Some are common, some energetic, some bring healing to mind and heart, but I encourage you to explore and bond with Mother Nature on a deeper level. They can provide a profound experience.

Here are a few tricks of the trade that will help extend the life of your cut flowers:

1. Cut the stems underwater, and at a slight angle rather than straight across. You can cut them in a bowl if that makes it easier.
2. Remove any leaves that will sit below the water level in the vase that will hold the flowers.
3. Avoid getting water on the petals.
4. Add 2 teaspoons of sugar to the water for food, and 1 teaspoon of vinegar to prevent bacteria from growing.
5. Every day or two, change the water in the vase and use the recipe listed in 4.

If you get flowers in florist foam rather than in a vase, you will need to alter the method slightly. Mix up water and the sugar and vinegar in a jug. Then pour this concoction into the foam.

When flowers are first cut, they can get tiny air bubbles trapped within the stem, which prevents them from absorbing water properly. This results in faster wilting. You can prevent this from happening by always re-cutting the stems once you get them home (even precut flowers from the grocery store).

African Violet; Agapanthus (Lily of the Nile); Anthurium (Flamingo Lily); Azalea; Baby's Breath; Begonia; Bird-of-Paradise; Bluebell; Bougainvillea; Bromeliad; Cactus; Calendula; Calla Lily; Cherry Blossom; Clover; Crab Apple; Crocus; Daisy; Dandelion; Dianthus; Echinacea (Purple Cornflower); Eucalyptus; Freesia; Fushsia; Geranium; Gerbera (African daisy); Heather; Hibiscus; Hyacinth; Hydrangea; Jasmine; Jonquil; Lantana; Lavender; Lilac; Lily (Orange); Lily (pink); Lily of the Valley; Lotus; Mandevilla; Moonflower; Passion-flower; Peony; Poinsettia;

Poppy; Portulaca; Scaevola; Snapdragon; Sweet Pea; Tulip; Wisteria.

Birth gives us our relatives, but choice gives us our flowers. Fate will not let us pick our relatives, but we are allowed to pick and select the flowers and our friends.

Robert Louis Stevenson said: *"So long as we love we serve; so long as we are loved by others, I would almost say that we are indispensable; and no man is useless while he has a friend. Or a Garden of the Heart.*

7 Feast Of The LORD Being Symbolic Of New Life

Below is an overview of how the festivals of our Heavenly Father is liken unto new life.

Feast	Christian Fulfillment	Baby Development
Passover (Pesach) Fertilization must take place within 24 hours.	**New Life (Egg)** Leviticus 23:5	**Ovulation**
Unleavened Bread Matzoh Bread is stripped	**The Seed (Planting)** 1 Corinthians 5:7-8 Leviticus 23:6-8	**Fertilization** Christ buried
First Fruits Spring planting Leviticus 23:10-11; (Matthew 27:27-53; Early crop of believers)	**Resurrection** Resurrection Day Resurrection of the entire church	**Raised from dead**
Pentecost Acts 2:1-50 days from Reed Sea. 50 days Embryo becomes a fetus. Pentecost Greek word means 50.	**Harvest**	**New Creature** Fetus Sweet Holy Spirit

The 4 feast (festivals) above have been fulfilled at Pentecost. Christ breathed the Holy Spirit upon the disciples.

The following 3 festivals are unfulfilled. We await their fulfillment.

Feast	Christian Fulfillment	Baby Development
Trumpets 1st day of 7th month the baby can hear.	**Catching Up (Rapture)** Joshua 6:5 1 Thessalonians 4:16-17	**Hearing**

Feast	Christian Fulfillment	Baby Development
Day of Atonement 10 days into 7th month fetal blood changes so that it can carry it's own oxygen.	**Redemption**	**Blood** Hemoglobin A
Tabernacles End of Feasts Leviticus 23:27 15th day of 7th month Normal baby has 2 healthy lungs	**Kingdom** House of Spirit Spirit in the Air	**Lungs** Baby will live if born at Tabernacles

---

| **Hanukkah** | **Eternity** | **Eternal Life** |

Not given by God. A days' supply of oil lasted 8 nights. It's beyond Tabernacles and beyond the Kingdom. We have eternity with God. This is the fulfillment.

Job 23:12;

12 "I don't withdraw from his lips' command; I treasure his words more than my daily food."

Ecclesiastes 12:13;

13 Now all has been heard; here is the conclusion of the matter: Fear God and keep his commandments, for this is the duty of all mankind. (NIV®)

SMILE... GOD LOVES YOU... KEEP LOOKING UP!

Made in the USA
Charleston, SC
01 June 2016